Curious Laddoos

Fun Answers to Big Questions about Hindu Life

Shruti Haldia Negi

Ananya Matta

BLUEROSE PUBLISHERS
India | U.K.

Copyright © Shruti Haldia Negi and Ananya Matta 2024

All rights reserved by author. No part of this publication may be reproduced, stored in a retrieval system or transmitted in any form or by any means, electronic, mechanical, photocopying, recording or otherwise, without the prior permission of the author. Although every precaution has been taken to verify the accuracy of the information contained herein, the publisher assume no responsibility for any errors or omissions. No liability is assumed for damages that may result from the use of information contained within.

BlueRose Publishers takes no responsibility for any damages, losses, or liabilities that may arise from the use or misuse of the information, products, or services provided in this publication.

For permissions requests or inquiries regarding this publication, please contact:

BLUEROSE PUBLISHERS
www.BlueRoseONE.com
info@bluerosepublishers.com
+91 8882 898 898
+4407342408967

ISBN: 978-93-6261-636-4
EISBN: 978-93-6261-148-2

First Edition: May 2024

Contents

Why do we have so many Gods and Goddesses?	4
Why do we worship idols?	6
Why do we light diyas?	7
Why do we apply tilak?	9
Why do we ring the temple bell?	11
Why do we offer prasada in temples?	13
Why do we do Parikrama?	15
Why is Ganeshji worshipped first at every puja?	16
Why do we worship cows?	18
Why do we remove our footwear before entering the temple?	20
Why do we chant AUM?	21
Why do we fast?	23
Why are we vegetarian?	25
Why do we offer water to the rising sun?	26
Why do we worship Tulsi plant?	28
Why do we touch the feet of parents and elderly relatives?	30
Why should we not step on books?	31
Why do we recite mantras?	32
Why is the Lotus considered sacred?	33
Why do we draw the Swastika?	35

Why do we have so many Gods and Goddesses?

Hinduism's many Gods and Goddesses are like different colors in a big box of crayons. Just as you choose the right crayon to create a specific drawing, people choose which God to connect with based on their needs and beliefs.

We believe there is one supreme power called "Brahma."

Brahma is like the box of crayons because it contains all the colors, representing the ultimate source of all Gods and Goddesses.

Each God or Goddess has a unique role, similar to different superheroes in a team, each with their own superpowers and responsibilities.

For example, think of Lord Vishnu as the one who takes care of everything in the universe, making sure everything is balanced.

Goddess Saraswati is like a great teacher who helps us learn new things and gives us wisdom.

Lord Ganesha is like a superhero who helps us get past any problems or obstacles we might face.

And Goddess Lakshmi is the one who brings us good luck and gives us wealth and prosperity.

Even though there are many Gods and Goddesses, they all come from the same source, which is Brahma. This way, people can connect with the divine in a way that feels right for them, just like choosing the crayon that best fits their drawing. It's a way to make the world more colorful and meaningful!

Why do we worship idols?

Think of a superhero action figure that you really like. You can see it, touch it, and it feels real to you. That's a bit like why we have idols when we worship.

Idols are like special action figures of gods and goddesses.

Firstly, idols make the divine more relatable–it's easier for our minds to connect with something we can see and touch. Gods sometimes take forms that look like ours, becoming superhero friends who understand us. Idols become symbols of hope, strength, and guidance – like having a friend in a godly form.

Idols also help us concentrate our thoughts during worship. Just like how you concentrate on your favorite toy while playing, idols become a focal point for our prayers and meditations.

You know how sometimes talk to our toys and imagine they're answering back? In the same way, praying to idols helps us feel close to God.

They keep God in our hearts, reminding us of how amazing God is and making us feel happy and peaceful.

Why do we light diyas?

Imagine the diya as a magical light in every Indian home, shining like a tiny beacon of tradition. A long time ago, people lit diyas to brighten up temples when there was no electricity, and now, it's become a special thing we do every day. The diya, like a little lamp, is lit twice a day—when the sun says good morning and when it bids us good night. Why? Because it's a way to show love and respect to our family deities, the special gods we believe in.

Now, here's the fascinating part: the diya isn't just a light; it's symbol for super-smart things—knowledge and inner wealth. You know, just like how light chases away darkness, knowledge chases away not-knowing things.

When we light the diya, it's like saying, 'Hey, knowledge, you're the best treasure!' It's a little ceremony to remind us that knowing things is super important for success outside and for feeling good inside.

Would you like to know the science behind it?

Lighting the diya makes our brains feel special. The light's magic waves make our brains more focused and attentive during special moments like prayers. And guess what else? The little particles that come out when the lamp burns act like tiny superheroes too—they clean up the air and make it pure. It's like inviting good vibes and making everything super clean and happy.

But the best part? The diya's job is to kick out darkness and bad vibes, not just from our homes but from our minds and hearts too. The flame is like a superhero friend, bringing in positive energy and making everything feel bright and pure.

So, when you see a diya, think of it as a tiny superhero light, spreading goodness and joy all around!

Why do we apply tilak?

Applying tilak, a special mark on the forehead, is an important tradition for Hindus. It's made from sacred things like ash, vermillion, or sandalwood paste, making it super special! Now, let's uncover why it's more than just a mark.

Firstly, tilak is believed to be a symbol for your third eye. You know, that imaginary eye on your forehead linked to super-smart thinking and spiritual awakenings. So, when you wear tilak, it's like having a secret code that connects you to amazing spiritual powers*.

Secondly, it acts like a magical shield! Tilak creates a force field around you, stopping any bad vibes from getting in. It becomes your own superhero protection against negativity. Especially when things get stressful, tilak is there to keep your mind calm and centered.

---

*Spiritual powers are special abilities that some people believe they have. These abilities might help them feel connected to the world around them in a special way.

Next up, tilak makes your brain super smart! When it's on your forehead, it activates a special energy center, making you super focused. It's like a magical boost for your brain, perfect for students, professionals, or anyone who needs to concentrate.

And guess what? It's not just about looking cool; tilak is a health superhero too! According to Ayurveda (that's a super ancient health science), wearing tilak helps balance your body's energy. Plus, the ingredients like sandalwood and turmeric make your skin healthy and happy.

Now, here's the fun part! Tilak is like a secret code at parties. When people see your tilak, they know you're part of an awesome tradition. It's like wearing a badge that says, 'I'm part of the cool tilak club!'

So, wearing tilak isn't just a tradition; it's a magical mark that connects you to cool powers, protects you, makes you super smart, keeps you healthy, and even gets you into the cool club!

Why do we ring the temple bell?

Imagine the temple bell as a magical instrument that makes the temple a happy place! When we ring it, something special happens.

Firstly, the bell's sound is like a beautiful melody that reaches out to God. It sends a message, saying, "Hey, God, we're here, and we want to be close to you!" The sound also whispers "Om," the sound of the Universe, making it a way to connect with God.

Secondly, when the bell rings, it creates vibrations that fill the temple with positive energy. The sound makes the temple feel alive and vibrant, creating a peaceful atmosphere where everyone can feel calm and happy.

Now, here's the fascinating part! The bell is made in a special scientific way that makes its sound very unique. The sound of the bell awakens our mind and helps us concentrate on our prayers. It's a gentle reminder to focus and connect with God in our hearts.

In a nutshell, ringing the temple bell is like sending a sweet song to God, a way of saying, "We're here and happy to be with you!" It's a joyful sound that brings good vibes, helps us concentrate on our prayers, and makes the temple a peaceful place for everyone. So, the next time you hear the bell, know that its sound is spreading love, positivity, and mindfulness all around!

Why do we offer prasada in temples?

Imagine visiting a temple as an exciting adventure where something magical happens! In temples, people offer special gifts to God, and one of these gifts is called "prasada."

Now, think of prasada like a treat that God shares with everyone. It starts with people offering God's favourite food as a way of saying, "Thank you for everything!" This is a big gesture of love and respect. Then, something incredible happens—God magically blesses the food!

The special food, now called prasada, becomes a yummy gift from God. It's not just regular food; it's filled with the magic of God's love and blessings. When people eat prasada, it's like taking a bite of happiness and goodness.

But here's the coolest part: prasada is not just about eating. It's also about sharing! When people share prasada with others, they spread happiness and magic, making everyone feel good inside. It brings everyone together, making them feel like one big happy family.

So, the next time you see someone sharing prasada in the temple, remember it's not just food; it's a magical treat from God that makes everyone happy and connected. It's a delicious snack that brings people closer and fills their hearts with joy!

Why do we do Parikrama?

Imagine going on a magical carousel ride around a temple! It's like stepping onto a special ride that draws a big, invisible circle with the temple's heart as the center – and this amazing journey is called "Parikrama."

Now, think of the temple as a place where we feel close to God. When we go around it on the carousel, we give God a big, invisible hug. But here's the really cool part: no matter where we start or who we are, we're always the same distance from God. It signifies that God is everywhere around us, showering love equally.

The best part is, when we go around the temple, we do it in a special way – always moving in a clockwise direction, just like the carousel goes round and round.

Going clockwise means we're saying, "God, you're at the center of everything we do and think!" We promise to live a good and kind life, just like a superhero following the path of goodness.

So, when you see people going around the temple on this magical carousel ride, remember it's not just a walk; it's a joyful journey of love and goodness. It's like a big, invisible hug for God, connecting everyone in a carousel of joy and kindness!

Why is Ganeshji worshipped first at every puja?

This has a delightful story behind it. Once there was a fascinating race between two special gods, Lord Ganesha and his big brother, Lord Kartikeya. The challenge was to go around the entire universe!

Now, Lord Kartikeya, with his speedy peacock, zoomed off to finish the race. But here's where it gets really interesting. Lord Ganesha, known for being super wise and devoted, had a different plan.

Instead of racing around the universe, Ganesha decided to go around his mom and dad – Lord Shiva and Parvati. When asked why, Ganesha shared something amazing. He believed his parents were like the whole universe to him. He thought going around them meant going around everything!

This special and loving choice touched Shiva and Parvati's hearts. They were so impressed by Ganesha's wisdom and love that they gave him the Fruit of Knowledge and the gift of living forever! And that's why, in every puja or ceremony, we start by worshiping Lord Ganesha. People believe that by doing this, they're asking for wisdom, success, and help in removing any obstacles.

Lord Ganesha is like our superhero for making things go smoothly. So, the tradition of worshipping Lord Ganesha first is a reminder of this beautiful story about love, wisdom, and starting things with a bit of magic!

Why do we worship cows?

Do you have a friend who is super kind, always sharing and never asking for anything in return? That's a bit like how Hindus see cows! We don't exactly worship cows, but we really, really respect and love them.

Cows are like superheroes in Hinduism, representing lots of cool things. First off, they're seen as a symbol of the Earth, like a giving and caring friend. Just as you might decorate your room for a special occasion, Hindus decorate and honor cows during festivals. But remember, they're not treating cows like gods; it's more like giving a big "thank you" to a friend.

Now, why do cows get all this attention? Well, it's because they're super awesome givers.

They provide milk, which is like a superhero drink for people, right? Cows only need water, grass, and grains, but in return, they give us milk that keeps us healthy and strong.

And do you know why most Hindus don't eat beef? It's because we want to show extra love and respect for these superhero cows. In Hindu stories, cows represent qualities like being gentle, strong, and always giving. It's like having a friend who teaches you to be kind and generous.

Gandhi, a very wise person, said that protecting cows is like protecting all the weak and helpless beings in the world. Hindus even have special festivals where we pamper cows with garlands and treats. It's like giving a big hug to these gentle friends.

So, why do we love and care for cows so much? It's because cows are like Earth's superheroes, teaching us about kindness, generosity, and being super awesome friends!

Why do we remove our footwear before entering the temple?

Think of a temple like a cozy home for God, just like your own home but extra special. You know how at home, everyone leaves their shoes at the door to keep things clean and show respect? Well, it's the same at God's home – the temple!

So, when we kick off our shoes before stepping into the temple, we are telling God, "Dear God, I'm leaving all the dirt and outside stuff right here. Now, I'm all set to fill my heart with love and goodness in your awesome home." It's our way of showing respect to God's house, just like we do at our own home.

And here's the cool part! This tradition goes way back in time. In the old stories, people believed that by leaving behind the dirt and worries of the world with their shoes, they could enter God's home with a clean and happy heart.

But wait, there's a science twist too! You see, shoes can carry germs and dirt from outside, and we definitely don't want to bring those into God's home. By leaving our shoes outside, we're not only showing love and respect but also helping to keep the temple a clean and healthy place. It's like making a double effort to show love to God's cozy home!

Why do we chant AUM?

In Hinduism, chanting Aum is like singing a super special song, but it's not just any song – it's a magical sound that represents the whole universe!

Imagine the universe like a giant storybook that has everything from the beginning to now and even what will happen in the future. Aum is like the music that tells this incredible story. When people chant Aum, they make three special sounds: 'A,' 'U,' and 'M.' Each sound is like a musical note with its own job in the story.

'A' is the starting sound, like the first chapter of a book. It's linked to the idea of creating things, like how an artist starts a beautiful painting. It's a happy and exciting sound, kind of like when you start a new adventure.

'U' is the middle sound, like the chapters in the middle of the story. It's a strong and steady sound that keeps the story going. It's like the hero of the story who protects everything and makes sure it stays amazing.

'M' is the ending sound, like the last chapter of a book. It represents finishing and starting something new. It's not sad; it's more like when you finish a great book and feel satisfied.

After these sounds, there's silence – the quiet part after the music stops. This silence is like the calm after a storm, or the peace after an exciting day. It's a reminder that things are always changing, and there's a magical cycle of new beginnings and peaceful endings.

People believe that chanting Aum brings good vibes and helps them connect with something bigger than themselves. It's like a special way of talking to the universe and being part of its incredible story!

Why do we fast?

Imagine fasting as a superhero, training for your body and mind! In Hinduism, fasting is a special timeout to get closer to the divine, not to make the gods happy, but to clean up our bodies and minds.

Now, think of fasting as a way to teach ourselves to be strong, like superheroes in training. It's like saying, "Hey, body and mind, let's see how strong and disciplined we can be!" Just like heroes face challenges, fasting helps us learn to handle difficulties and stay focused.

And guess what? Fasting isn't just about getting superhero strength; it's also a health boost! It helps with weight management, keeps our blood sugar in check, makes our hearts strong, and even helps our brains work better. So, it's like giving our bodies a spa day to feel fantastic!

In Hinduism, people fast on special days or during festivals. It's a way to show dedication to the gods and give our bodies a break. Some fast by not eating anything, while others give up certain foods. It's like choosing different levels of superhero training based on what feels right for you.

Even our ancient medicine, Ayurveda, supports fasting for keeping our bodies healthy. It's a traditional health secret that's been around for over 5,000 years!

But here's the coolest part: fasting also makes us think about others. Feeling a bit hungry during fasting makes us understand what it's like for people who don't have enough to eat. We become superheroes with big hearts, caring about everyone around us!

So, fasting in Hinduism is not just a practice; it's a superhero workout for our bodies, minds, and hearts!

Why are we vegetarian?

Hindus often choose not to eat meat for some cool reasons:

1. Being Kind to Animals: We believe in being super kind to animals, like cows, chickens, and others. We like to be friends with all creatures and not hurt them.

2. Keeping Karma Positive: We think every action has a consequence, and eating meat might bring not-so-happy results. So, by not eating animals, we hope for good vibes and happiness.

3. Feeling Healthy and Happy: Eating lots of veggies and fruits makes us feel strong, happy, and healthy. It's a superhero diet that keeps us fit and ready for anything!

4. Protecting Nature: Choosing not to eat meat is a superhero move to protect nature. It helps keep forests, rivers, and the Earth healthy. Imagine being a superhero for the planet!

So, being vegetarian for Hindus is a mix of being kind to animals, keeping karma positive, feeling healthy, and protecting the Earth – just like superheroes on a mission!

Why do we offer water to the rising sun?

Offering water to the rising sun, known as Surya Arghya, is a special morning tradition to greet the Sun God.

Let's understand why we do it:

1. Sun's Goodness: Early sunlight has essential vitamins that makes us strong, just like having a healthy breakfast but from the sun!

2. Eye Care: Looking at the sun rays through the stream of water while pouring keeps our eyes healthy and clear.

3. Barefoot Happiness: Standing barefoot in the grass feels like a natural foot massage. It's good for our feet and makes them feel happy!

4. Ankle Exercise: Standing on our tiptoes while pouring water is an exercise for our ankles. It keeps them strong and pain-free.

5. Vitamin D Boost: After a morning bath, our skin absorbs the sun's vitamins better. It's a way of giving our body an extra boost of goodness.

6. Fresh Air: Doing this in the morning lets us breathe in fresh and clean air, like taking a big breath of nature's own oxygen.

7. Mindful Moment: Chanting Surya Mantra during this time is a great exercise for our minds. It helps us stay focused and calm for the day.

8. Sun's Energy: The sun gives us energy, and by doing this, we say, "Thanks, Sun, for being a special part of our lives!"

How to do it:
- ✓ Wake up early and take a refreshing bath.
- ✓ Find a clear spot with a good view of the rising sun.
- ✓ Stand barefoot and pour water from a special cup, saying special words and looking at the sun through the stream of water.

So, offering water to the rising sun is a lovely morning tradition that keeps our bones, eyes, feet, and minds happy and ready for the day!

Why do we worship Tulsi plant?

Meet our green superhero, Tulsi! Every Hindu home has this special plant, and it's not just any plant – it's like having a magical friend who brings happiness and blessings. Let's explore why Tulsi is so important:

1. Home for Goddess Lakshmi: We believe that Goddess Lakshmi, the goddess of wealth and happiness, loves to stay in the Tulsi plant. So, by taking care of Tulsi, we make our homes a happy place.

2. Morning Plant Party: Every morning, we have a special party for Tulsi. We say nice things, sing songs, and make Tulsi feel loved. It's like a morning hug for our green friend.

3. Thirsty Tulsi: Tulsi gets a drink of water after our morning party. Just like we need water, Tulsi feels happy with some water too.

4. Lamp of Happiness: In the evening, after our evening rituals, we light a lamp under Tulsi. It's like saying, "Tulsi, thank you for being our happiness superhero!" It makes our home glow with joy.

5. Special Days for Tulsi: Tulsi is so special that we don't water it on Sundays and Ekadashi. We also don't pluck its leaves on these days. It's like giving Tulsi a little break.

6. Magic Problem Solver: We believe that when we love and worship Tulsi, it helps make our lives better by bringing positivity and removing obstacles.

7. Tulsi's Song: After all the love, we sing a special song for Tulsi, thanking her for being our friend and bringing happiness to our home.

So, worshipping Tulsi is not just a boring plant task; it's like having a green superhero friend that makes our homes happy and full of blessings!

Why do we touch the feet of parents and elderly relatives?

Ever heard of Charan Sparsh? It's a magical greeting, a positive energy exchange, a friendly exercise, and a cool move. It's our special way of showing love and respect to our elders. Here's why it's fantastic:

Charan Sparsh is a combination of two words - Charan, which means feet, and Sparsh, which means to touch. So, when we do Charan Sparsh, we touch the feet of our elders. It's a bit like saying, "You're awesome, and I respect you a lot!"

Our bodies have energy, right? When we touch their feet, it's like giving and receiving a high-five of positive energy. This is what makes this special greeting so cool!

Now, think of it as a friendly exercise. When we do Charan Sparsh, we bend a little, stretch our hands, and it keeps us feeling strong and healthy. It is just like a dance move that also makes us feel great!

Guess what? After our move, elders give us pats on the head. By doing that, they pass on wisdom, success, and all the good stuff! It is also a way of saying, "You're awesome, and I'm here to support you!"

So, next time you greet your parents, grandparents or any elderly relatives, don't forget to do the Charan Sparsh!

Why should we not step on books?

In our culture, there's a rule that says we shouldn't step on books or touch them with our feet. Why?

Think of it as a secret code of respect. Just like you wouldn't want anyone to mistreat your favorite toy or even your favorite friends, people don't want to mistreat their books because they're like magical doors to a world of cool stuff.

Now, there's a super awesome goddess called Saraswati. She's the boss of all things smart and knowledgeable. When we touch books with our feet, it's like saying something not nice to her, and we definitely don't want to do that!

It's not just about books; it's also about treating people with kindness. Imagine if someone stepped on your foot – ouch, right? So, we try not to touch anyone, especially elders, with our feet.

Now what did we learn? We should not be stepping on books or touching people with our feet. It is all about being kind, showing respect to smart stuff, and keeping our awesome goddess Saraswati happy!

Why do we recite mantras?

Reciting mantras is like giving your mind and body a happy boost! Let's see the cool things it brings to the party:

1. Happy Breaths: Think of each mantra like a little sip of yummy lemonade. When you say them, it's like taking a sip that calms your mind and makes your body feel great!

2. Cheerful Tunes: Mantras are like musical notes that create a happy tune around you. The more you say them, the more joyful vibes you spread, making everything around you feel like a happy dance party.

3. Brain Exercise: Saying mantras is like sending your brain to a workout. It stretches and strengthens your mind, making it super sharp. So, when you have puzzles or school stuff, your mind is all set for a fantastic show!

4. Peaceful Mind Garden: Imagine your mind as a garden. Saying mantras is like planting beautiful flowers in it. It turns your mind into a peaceful and calm place, perfect for chilling out.

5. Pocket-Sized Superpower: The coolest part? You can carry this superpower with you! Even if you're playing or having snacks, just listening to mantras can add a sprinkle of magic to your day.

Why is the Lotus considered sacred?

Meet the lotus, the most blessed flower in Hindu stories! It's not just a regular flower; it has special qualities:

Wonder 1: Beauty and Riches!
The lotus brings good luck, comfort, and happiness. It's like a magical flower that spreads beauty and richness to everyone around.

Wonder 2: Incredible Life Journey!
Picture this – the lotus grows in muddy water but turns into something stunning and clean. It teaches us the story of rising above challenges and becoming something extraordinary and wonderful.

Wonder 3: Yoga Pose Magic!
In yoga, people do a pose named after the lotus. It's like a cool move for the mind, making it super calm and focused. The lotus is a yoga superstar!

Wonder 4: Goddess Connection!
Even goddesses in Hindu stories adore the lotus! Goddess Lakshmi, the one who brings wealth and money, sits on a lotus. It's her special throne, like a unique seat.

Wonder 5: Heart's Special Power!
Imagine having a tiny guiding light in your heart. In meditation, people think of a lotus inside, and in its center, there's a little light – the power of the true self.

So, the lotus isn't just a flower; it's a marvel with qualities of beauty, strength, and even a special guiding seat in your heart!

Why do we draw the Swastika?

Once upon a time, in the colorful land of Hindu traditions, there was a tiny but mighty symbol named Swastika. This symbol wasn't just ordinary; it was like a magical charm filled with superpowers.

During special celebrations and prayers, people would draw the Swastika, activating its first superpower – Luck Unleashed! It was like turning on a charm that brought good luck and spread happiness to everyone nearby.

But wait, there's more! During festivals, homes got a festive makeover with Swastikas at the door. It was like having a superhero friend guarding the house, welcoming in good vibes and prosperity. The Swastika became a Festival Friend, making celebrations even more special.

Now, here's the exciting part – the Swastika wasn't alone in its adventures. It had a superhero sidekick, none other than Lakshmi Devi, the goddess of wealth. Drawing the Swastika was like sending an invitation to this superhero friend, bringing joy and riches along. What an amazing team!

 People didn't just draw Swastikas on paper; they created magical symbols on their hands, walls, pots, and even on the floor during prayers. It was like casting spells of positivity and creating a superhero aura around them.

And do you know the Swastika's secret identity? Its name! Swastika's name is like a magic spell itself, coming from Sanskrit, a super ancient language. It means something like "encouraging being," adding an extra layer of superhero magic.

So, the next time you see a Swastika, remember it's not just lines on paper; it's a superhero symbol that brings good vibes, happiness, and even calls on a goddess friend for a magical visit!

www.ingramcontent.com/pod-product-compliance
Lightning Source LLC
LaVergne TN
LVHW061627070526
838199LV00070B/6614